Do You Have a Dream Workbook

5 Keys to Realize Your Dream

GRACE ALLISON

Do You Have a Dream?

Copyright © 2018, Grace Allison. All Rights Reserved.

No part of this publication may be reproduced, stored in a retrieval system or transmitted, in any form or by any means – electronic, mechanical, photocopying, recording or otherwise – without prior written permission from the publisher, except for the inclusion of brief quotations in a review.

For information about this title or to order other books and/or electronic media, contact the publisher:

Modern Mystic Media
www.ModernMysticMedia.com
Grace@ModernMysticMedia.com

Library of Congress Control Number: 2004090310

ISBN: 978-0-9988308-0-3

Printed in the United States of America

Cover and Interior design: 1106 Design, LLC

DEDICATION

To all brave dreamers who have a courageous heart to walk the path of the Spiritual Warrior

WHAT I DO

I am married to Dr. John Blair, PhD, professor emeritus from the Rawls College of Business at Texas Tech University. In 2011, after being single for thirty years, I found a good man who gave me the respect and loving I deserved. When I married John, I retired from forty years of the world of business, marketing, and business development. Now I take care of my husband, write books, play golf, travel, and serve my community.

Each morning when we rise, John and I drink our morning coffee and watch the morning news. I do my yoga practice, breathing, and stretching to get my body ready for the day. Next, I prepare breakfast. On most days, I take time to do spiritual exercises. I feel scattered when I do not keep my morning ritual.

By mid-morning, I am on social media, followed by either writing or playing golf. Daily chores of grocery shopping, laundry, and cleaning house keep our household in good order.

I am an autodidact who is curious and loves to learn. Writing was a large part of my business world. With retirement, I have time to use my creative writing skills. In the last ten years, I have taken courses on writing fiction and nonfiction, publishing, and marketing.

Currently I have one book, *A Dream Is a Wish the Heart Makes: Or If at First You Don't Succeed, Change the Rules*, which won the Bronze E-Global Book Award and is available at bookstores and online.

I am writing my novel, *Einstein's Compass: A Novel of What If?* with my friend of forty years, Laren Bright, a three-time Emmy-nominated writer. He and I share similar spiritual teachings through the Movement of Spiritual Inner Awareness. Through my forty years of being a student of MSIA, I have been inspired to share the world of the Mystical Travelers. This novel featuring the Mystical Travelers is a science-fiction thriller: "What if Einstein met spiritual beings who assisted him in creating his miracle theory?"

Once a month, I advertise online through the community network "Meetup." I offer a free spiritual awareness class in my home. Through techniques of breathing and going inward, we exercise the living spirit within the spiritual heart, where we explore the inner mysteries of light. Recently, I volunteered my "Meetup" format with the coordinator of MSIA's Home Seminar Administrator. Together, we created a format for home seminar leaders around the world.

> *"Amateurs sit and wait for inspiration; the rest of us just get up and go to work."*
> — STEPHEN KING

WHAT I KNOW

Through hard lessons of trying to be a good person and strive for success, I discovered a simple rule: "Take care of yourself *first*, so you can take care of others."

I am a natural caregiver. My father was an abusive alcoholic; my mother and sister died by suicide and suffered from mental illness. At ten years old and the oldest of four children, I became the responsible one in the family. By the time I was in my late twenties, I was broken and exhausted from giving to those around me. As an empath, I see and feel into people's needs. I have had to learn to discriminate and create boundaries to not rescue people.

The fact is, our planet is a place of learning through change—always has been, always will be. Today with global connectivity, social media, and a million ways to distract themselves, people are grasping for instant answers to their life's dilemmas. As a wellness coach, I hear the cries of "rescue me" with *the* pill, diet, or fast solution to shelter themselves from the change of the physical world that will magically give them all the world's treasures.

As a wellness coach, when I work with people who want to feel better, I put the responsibility of their wellness in their hands by asking, "If you had all the health, energy, and happiness, what would you be doing with your life?"

There are as many thought leaders in the world as there are students. I encourage anyone who is ready to take charge of their lives and have no idea how, to just pick one. I did when I had to. When I had cancer, was without a job, and was lost, I had to—to save my own life.

"I dream for a living."
STEVEN SPIELBERG

WHAT I WANT

What Is a "Modern Mystic"?

During the fifteenth century, the Spanish Inquisition punished people who had otherworldly experiences with God. Anyone who was a healer or had intuitive knowing of God was burned at the stake. According to the church, the only way a person could hear the word of God was through a priest or minister. Today, the term "mystic" is associated with the occult, magic, astrology, and tarot readings. I want to educate people to know that the mystical is not dark magic nor should it be ostracized.

Being a mystic is a spiritual, religious, and transcendental experience. St. Theresa of Avila, a former Jewess, was a Catholic nun and a mystic in the sixteenth century. The Catholic Church has venerated more than 10,000 saints, with many being mystics. Patron saints are often chosen today because an interest, talent, or event in their lives overlaps with the special area. For example, St. Francis of Assisi was a mystic who loved nature, and so he is the patron of ecologists. St. Francis de Sales was a mystical writer, and so he is the patron of journalists and writers. St. Clare of Assisi is a mystic and the patron of television because one Christmas when she was too ill to leave her bed, she saw and heard Christmas Mass—even though it was taking place miles away. Angels are also named as patron saints.

I do not claim to be a saint. However, there are saints among us who do the work of loving service. In 1973, I discovered a spiritual phenomenon called Mystical Traveler Consciousness. Stepping into living love of the Mystical Traveler is like having a flashlight in the darkness of the soul. With the Light of God through exercising the living spirit within, you can step into an awareness that will lift and assist you in your life's lessons.

Let go of the world around you, go inside, find your dream, and follow the adventure of making it come true.

In your day-to-day learning, if you find a unique way of dreaming, pass it on. We on planet Earth are students of life. Maybe you can share and become a thought leader, too.

CONTENTS

SECTION I
If at First You Don't Succeed, Change the Rules 1

SECTION II
Do You Need to be Rescued? 13

SECTION III
Do You Believe in God? 27

SECTION IV
Emotions = Energy in Motion 45

SECTION V
What Are Boundaries? 63

SECTION VI
What Are Priorities? 81

SECTION VII
What Is the Value of Prayer? 89

SECTION VIII
IMAGE 115

SECTION IX
My Name Is I AM 149

SECTION X
Five Keys to Realizing Your Dream 167

Testimonial 171

About the Author 185

It is not the strongest or the most intelligent who will survive but those who can best manage change

CHARLES DARWIN

SECTION I

If at First You Don't Succeed, Change the Rules

Fear is challenging each person to awaken to their loving inside. Some of us are being tested with lost jobs or dying family members, maybe your home has been destroyed in a natural disaster, or perhaps, like me, you have had toxic family issues and serious illness. These are all part of the greater change that God is delivering to each person. It is a time of reassessment and inner discovery. Change can be scary, but it does not have to be. God is calling us to be more accountable in our relationships with each other and ourselves. We have opportunities and choices to make. Will we respond to our opportunities with love or with fear?

1

Fear is challenging each person to awaken to their loving inside. Let go and say, "Yes" to life, not "No."

2

Learn to trust. Find your spiritual knowing inside. There is a Higher Power that has insight and knowledge.

3

Become a spiritual scientist. Energy follows thought; imagine and feel your reality.

4

Change: do you like it? Will you respond to your opportunities with love or with fear?

....

....

....

....

....

....

....

5

Shift your inner resources from feeling out of control to experiencing inner freedom, inner strength, confidence, and love.

6

God is calling us to be more accountable in our relationships. We have opportunities and choices to make.

7

Trust your intuition and its symbols; value your creativity. Experience your soul's dreams, stories, and myths.

8

Honor your healing and prophetic qualities that have guided human beings through the ages.

9

Shift from a God of law to a God of grace. Discover that God is for you and not against you. God of Grace and mercy.

10

The kingdom of heaven is within each person. Everyone, not just the priests and ministers, has access to His divine guidance.

*We are our own dragons
as well as our own heroes,
and we have to rescue
ourselves from ourselves*

TOM ROBBINS

SECTION II

Do You Need to Be Rescued?

The need to be rescued is a cultural phenomenon that affects many areas of our society today. We are in a severe state of neediness and incompleteness that has rendered us spiritually impoverished. Not everyone is aware of their neediness. Jesus described those who are aware of their neediness as poor in spirit. The Greek word for "poor in spirit" is *ptochos*, which means a cringing beggar, dependent on others for survival. Jesus said, "Blessed are the poor in spirit, for theirs is the kingdom of heaven" (Matthew 5:3). Our state of incompleteness drives us outside of ourselves to God as the source of healing and hope.

Broken-heartedness is related to spiritual poverty. It is the state of being wounded or crushed by some loss, person, hurt, injustice, or circumstance. When a person is downcast because of an emotional, relational, or career injury, they can be brokenhearted. God has a special tenderness for this condition. Broken-heartedness often brings about a sense of spiritual poverty as it shows us our need. This dark night of the soul of deep need stems from experiences of feeling unworthy, ashamed, or guilty. It can feel like a cold, blustery wind blowing inside. Who or what will rescue me from this pain? What will fill this empty, cold darkness? To feel so tortured can be like living in hell. What will cover and soothe the inner pain? Some people will eat; others will drink alcohol or use drugs. Some escape with risky sexual behavior, credit cards, gambling, and spending money beyond their means or working long hours without a day off or holiday. All of these addictive, fear-based behaviors are choices based on our inner lack and the want to be rescued.

The need to be rescued by someone or something outside of ourself is responsible for codependent, addictive, and often abusive relationships, as well as for financial and health problems. A constant need creates difficulty in all aspects of our life. For example, imagine you have a job, but you need money. You are really scared. The job you have is not the one you really want, but it pays the bills. Maybe you think having money will make you feel more secure about yourself. In your mind, you rationalize (rational lies) how great you will feel and what you will get from the situation.

Have you ever heard the statement, "As a man thinketh in his heart, he becomes"? What we focus on and put energy into is what we get.

Spiritual poverty is a rich part of the growth process. The more broken we are, the more God can grow us up. What do we need to be happy and well adjusted? The basic needs for anyone are food, shelter, air, and love. Even having those things, most people still feel need or lack. You may covet many things, particularly material objects and experiences (a car, boat, a stereo, money, sex, or maybe chocolate ice cream).

Healthcare providers, like doctors, nurses, firefighters, and emergency-care people, are here to rescue us but only over the short term, until we can get past the injury so we can go on with our lives. Ministers and priests are here to assist us in our lives as counselors. Mothers, fathers, and family members are to show their love and wisdom. No one can make another person feel or change. There is no perfect life. We are just being human. So who is really in charge of us?

11

Blessed are the poor in spirit, for theirs is the kingdom of heaven. God is the source of healing and hope.

12

Broken-heartedness is related to spiritual poverty. Who or what will rescue me from my pain?

13

A dark night of the soul of need stems from experiences of feeling unworthy, shameful, or guilty.

14

What will fill this empty,
cold darkness? To feel
so tortured can be
like living in hell.

15

People will eat; others will drink alcohol or use drugs. Some escape with risky sexual behavior.

16

Addictive, fear-based behaviors are choices based on our inner want to be rescued.

17

Spiritual poverty is a rich part of the growth process. The more broken we are, the more God can grow us up.

18

What do we need to be happy and well adjusted? The basic needs for any one are food, shelter, air, and love.

19

Have you gone to the grocery store when you were hungry and bought a lot because your hunger made unnecessary things look good?

....

....

....

....

....

20

The need to be rescued is responsible for codependent, addictive and often abusive relationships.

Do not let your hearts be troubled. Trust in God; trust also in me.

JESUS CHRIST

SECTION III

Do You Believe in God?

One of the biggest obstacles of growth is our view of God. The first aspect of that shift has to be the shift from a God of law to a God of grace. People must discover that God is for them and not against them. This is what it means to have a God of grace and a God of mercy. Jesus had a mission to show people what God was really like. "Immanuel," one of the names given to Jesus, means, "God with us." Moreover, when Jesus walked the earth, He showed us a very different God than we might expect. The kingdom of heaven is within each person; everyone, not just the priests and ministers, has access to His divine guidance.

Everything starts out with God as the Source. This is point number one in the Bible. Nothing was created before God, and everything that exists came from Him. This includes all the "stuff" of life: the resources, the principles, the purposes, the meaning—everything!

After making the "stuff," God made humankind and breathed life into them (Genesis 2:7). We have to understand this means to receive the Holy Spirit into the troubled areas of our lives. God is not only Creator but also re-creator of life. It becomes the system of how one overcomes depression, heals a marriage, or rescues a failing business career.

God's role is to provide, and our role is to receive. Our role is to be a dependent one. Independence is not an option for us. God existed without us, not vice versa. God's role is to be in control; our role is to surrender to God's control of the world, and we are to control our self.

It is difficult for some of us to imagine how God's creative energy works inside our mind, heart, and subconscious. To do so, imagine Eden. Eden was a sacred place. The experience of living in the garden was peace, reverence, joy, serenity, bliss, and love.

21

"God created the heavens and the earth. Everything starts out with God as the Source."

22

After making the "stuff," God made humankind and breathed life into them (Genesis 2:7).

23

God is not only Creator but recreator of life. Overcome a depression, heal a marriage, or rescue a failing business career.

24

God's role is to provide,
and our role is to receive.
Our role is to be a
dependent. Independence
is not an option for us.

25

God's role is to be in control; our role is to surrender to God's control of the world — we are to control our self.

26

Imagine living in a garden with peace, reverence, joy, serenity, bliss, and love.

27

Imagine the Garden of Eden. Picture how God's creative energy works inside our mind, heart, and subconscious.

28

Let go of any mental or emotional baggage at this time. Give it up to God and the Holy Spirit inside of you.

29

An aura is an invisible atmosphere supposedly surrounding a person or thing.

30

Continue with this process;
experience the resistance
to your dream each day
for at least 30 days.

31

This aura of invisible light is what I call our "ten acres" of energy. We are holy temples of God's loving light or energy.

32

We must honor and take care of our personal ten acres known as our Garden of Eden.

33

We stand on our own ground, aware of God's light. Eden can be a pleasant, harmonious, productive state of consciousness.

34

We can experience being in Eden when in a state of bliss in a harmonious body.

35

The garden is the spiritual body in which man dwells when he brings forth his thoughts after the original divine ideas.

Every intention sets energy into motion. Whether you are conscious of it or not.

GARY ZUKAV

SECTION IV

Emotions = Energy in Motion

During the course of any normal day, we think, say, and do many things. The words we say and their intent have the greatest influence on how we direct our lives. In our fast-paced society, we ignore or forget how powerful words can be. Words evoke emotions, trigger memories, and generate visceral reactions. Learning how to direct the mind and emotions is like the ability to turn darkness into light. Your attitude plays back information and needs to be checked over regularly.

Emotions = energy in motion. People who live their lives allowing their mind and emotions to run their lives are like ships on the ocean without a mast or a rudder. They are subject to the prevailing winds (thought) and water (emotion) of the moment. These people are outwardly seeking happiness and excitement by going from one person or idea to another, where their moods swing from feeling high to the great depths of depression. Trying to please everyone, with no direction and no way of knowing what is real, they put out false images of what people want them to be. With no boundaries to define themselves, nothing is ever misunderstood.

Feelings signal our state of being. Feelings tell us how we are doing, what matters to us, what needs changing, what is going well, and what is going badly. We are responsible for our own feelings. To disown our feelings and ignore responsibility for them is one of the most destructive things we can do both to others and to ourselves. When we take responsibility for our own disappointments, we are setting clear boundaries.

Think of driving your car. When you turn the key, the energy of the car starts. When you put the car in gear, your car is ready to drive into motion. Our body is much like a car. You think of something, and then your emotions come in to match the thought. When your emotions are in gear from reacting from fear or anger in a situation, you can really get carried away—the next thing you know, you are an accident waiting to happen. Awareness can be seeing your emotions from a place of "out of gear." Just neutrally observe how you feel about a situation before you put your emotions into gear. Slow down. Instead of going ninety miles an hour with your mind and emotions, try thirty-five miles an hour for a while. Instead of reacting to a situation through fear, stop, take a deep breath, and think about the situation; see if you can come up with at least three different ways to respond before speaking. This way, you are embracing your inner thoughts and feelings by using discernment and wisdom. Ask yourself, "How will I feel about the outcome of this situation in a week or two?"

36

The words we say and their intent evoke emotions, trigger memories, and generate visceral reactions.

37

Learning how to direct the mind and emotions is like the ability to turn darkness into light.

38

Emotions = energy in motion. Your attitude plays back information and needs to be checked over regularly.

39

People who allow their mind and emotions to run their lives are like ships on the ocean without a mast or a rudder.

40

Some people are subject to the prevailing winds (thought) and water (emotion) of the moment.

41

People without boundaries go from one person to another; moods swing from feeling high to the great depths of depression.

42

Feelings tell us how we are doing, what matters to us, what needs changing, what is going well, and what is going badly.

43

We are responsible for our own feelings. When we take responsibility for ourselves, we set clear boundaries.

44

Our body is much like a car. When you turn the key, the energy of the car starts. Emotions = energy in motion.

45

Emotions are in gear from reacting in fear or anger; the next thing you know, you are an accident waiting to happen.

46

Awareness is neutrally observing your emotions from a place "out of gear."

47

Instead of reacting through fear, stop and take a deep breath. Come up with at least three ways to respond before speaking.

48

Embrace your inner awareness. Ask yourself, "How will I feel about the outcome of this situation in a week?"

....

....

....

....

....

....

*Boundaries are
part of self-care.
They are healthy,
normal, and necessary.*

DOREEN VIRTUE

SECTION V

What are boundaries?

What would happen if you were driving down the interstate highway and there were no white lines on the highway—you can drive at any speed and in any direction. What a wild, chaotic mess! With time as their enemy, that is how some people live their lives. A person who lives their life without priorities or boundaries is constantly running from one emergency to another, out of control, using everyone and everything in their obsessive game of power and control until one day, they have a heart attack, car accident, lose their job, or worse, their life.

When we think of boundaries, we think of limits. Boundaries give us a sense of what is part of us and what is not part of us, what we will allow and what we won't, and what we will choose to do and what we choose not to do. My boundaries look like ten acres of land I call my Garden of Eden. My Garden is protected by an invisible energy field called an aura. 1 ❤ We all have this energy field around us. Remember being in an elevator and feeling the person next to you, but you really didn't touch them? That is what I call my "ten acres" of energy; it is an aura of invisible light. It is important to honor your own personal ten acres and care for it.

1 ❤ as defined in *The Auric Mirror* by Ella Vivian Power

Our attitudes are our opinions about something. We are responsible for our own attitudes, for they exist inside our "property line," our Garden of Eden. They are within our hearts, not someone else's. God tells us to examine and take responsibility for the attitudes and beliefs that govern our lives. They form the structure of our personality. In the beginning of life, we "soak up" attitudes; as we mature, we need to take responsibility for making sure our opinions are ours and not someone else's. We choose them.

Honoring our self and honoring other people as separate from us is also an aspect of boundaries. Separateness is an important aspect of human identity. How can we be connected to others without losing our identity and individuality? We are to master the art of "being me without losing you." Without boundaries, people are needy and demand a lot of attention.

When there are unclear boundaries in any relationship, anger and resentment occur as each person projects their unfulfilled need to be taken care of onto the other person. Developing our separateness involves knowing what our boundaries are. Knowing these boundaries helps us develop our separate and unique personalities.

"Treat others the same way you want them to treat you."

LUKE 6:31

Be courteous and have good manners. Always treat a human being as a person, that is, as an end in themselves and not merely a means to an end. Strive to impart dignity and self-worth to all you meet. Your character is shown in many ways, but one of the most obvious is the way you treat people. You will grow in character and reputation if you treat others with kindness.

49

Imagine driving down the interstate highway with no white lines on the highway, driving at any speed and in any direction.

....

....

....

....

....

....

50

People without priorities or boundaries are constantly running from one emergency to another, out of control.

51

When we think of boundaries, we think of limits. Boundaries give us a sense of what is part of us and what is not part of us.

52

Boundaries are like ten acres of land called the Garden of Eden, protected by an invisible energy field called an aura.

53

We all have an aura. Imagine being in an elevator and feeling the person next to you, but you really didn't touch them.

54

Surrounding you is your invisible aura. Honor your Garden of Eden and care for it.

55

We are responsible for our own attitudes, for they exist inside our "property line," our Garden of Eden.

56

God tells us to examine and take responsibility for the attitudes and beliefs that govern our lives.

57

In life, we "soak up" attitudes; as we mature, we take responsibility for our opinions and not someone else's.

58

Honoring our self and honoring other people as separate from us is also an aspect of boundaries.

59

Separateness is a part of human identity. How can we be connected to others without losing our identity and individuality?

60

Strive to impart dignity and self-worth to all you meet. Character is shown in the way you treat people.

61

You will grow in character and reputation if you treat others with kindness.

62

Imagine that you are standing in your Garden of Eden. What does it look like? Where is it? Who is with you?

I believe there are three keys to success. For me it is keeping my priorities in order: It's my faith and my family, and then the business.

KATHY IRELAND

SECTION VI

What Are Priorities?

Now take some time and honestly look at your priorities. Listed below are ten activities. Rank them in the order of their importance in your life, with one being the most important and ten the least important. If there are any additional activities not listed, write them in.

- Play
- Work
- School
- Friends
- Children
- God/Prayer
- Food/Nutrition
- Community Service
- Spouse
- Rest/Sleep

I believe in the Golden Rule, which means to love God with all your body, mind, and soul and your neighbor as yourself. That means to me that I must love myself and take care of myself *first* before I can really take care of others. My priorities look like this:

- God/Prayer
- Food/Nutrition
- Sleep/Rest
- Spouse
- Children
- Work
- Play
- Friends
- Community Service
- School

Now, compare your list of priorities and lifestyle to the one shown above. How are they different? How are they similar?

While it is fine to put other things before God, you may not experience the oneness you are thirsting for.

63

The Golden Rule means to love God with all your body, mind, and soul and your neighbor as yourself.

64

Love yourself and take care of yourself first, before you take care of others.

65

Priorities: God/prayer, food/nutrition, sleep/rest, spouse, children, work, play, friends, community service, school.

66

While it is fine to put other things before God, you may not experience the oneness you are thirsting for.

67

If having God is an issue, then use the practice of Gratitude. Begin your day with 3 things you are grateful for.

Prayer is the medium of miracles; in whatever way works for you, pray right now.

MARIANNE WILLIAMSON

SECTION VII

What Is the Value of Prayer?

It takes practice to become more at-one, more honest, more in-tune with yourself. To begin a life of living more with God and His loving, there are three basic principles: discipline, devotion, and introspection.

Our personality requires discipline for self-control; otherwise, our physical desires, the unquenchable thirst for food, sex, love, and other worldly objects, gets out of control as we try to possess and control things and people. Making a commitment at an appointed time every day to go inside and make contact with God through prayer and introspection builds confidence, detachment from worldly objects, inner strength, and compassion, enabling us to give of our self to the world.

Devotion is love. We need devotion to establish a way of life in which we let go of the physical world and walk in the presence of God, reminding us of the first commandment requiring us to love God with all our heart, all our soul, and all our mind. Sometimes I think we give as much of our heart, soul, and mind as possible to our fellow human beings, while trying hard not to forget God. This way, we can at least say we are not forgetting God. Nevertheless, Jesus' claim is much more radical. He asks for single-minded commitment to God and God alone. God wants all of our heart, all of our mind, and all of our soul. It is this unconditional and unreserved love for God that leads to the care for our neighbor: not as an activity which distracts us from God or competes with our attention for God, but as an expression of our love for God, who reveals Himself to us as the God of all people. When we go inside, we are in devotion, a humbleness of the spirit appears, and a connectedness to the Holy Spirit begins to take place. All of our anxieties, depressions, and worries of the world are gone and replaced with a tender loving.

God is not the bellhop in the sky to deliver every whim or wish. To let go and let God is to let go of the false pride of "I Know" to surrendering the rationalizing (rationing lies) of your life to the truth of what is really going on. This takes great courage and maturity. Prayer is a personal encounter and a transforming one. Do not resist your negative thoughts and feelings — they will just continue to grow; instead, embrace them by calling in God's loving light for the highest good and ask God to show you what to do and what the lesson might be that you are learning. Then let God know how grateful you are for His loving guidance and for all the gifts, talents, people, and things you have in the material world. He truly does love everyone and is just waiting to pour out more of His abundance if only we would become a disciple through disciplining our self in daily prayer.

God does more than hear words. He reads our hearts. Jesus taught that all good and bad originates in men's hearts. "A good man out of the good treasure of his heart bringeth forth that which is good; and an evil man out of the evil treasure of his heart bringeth forth that which is evil; for the abundance of the heart his mouth speaketh." (Luke 6:45)

Although my audience for this book and manual is predominately for Christians, I recognize and honor the different religious paths. As human beings in a sophisticated society, each culture has its own beliefs, with each saying your way is different from my way, your savior is not my savior; your forever is not my forever, etc. However, the truth is, all life is one life. There is only one game in progress. This is one race, with many different shades. We argue the name of God, what building, what day, what ritual. What do His stories mean? Truth is truth. If you hurt someone, you hurt yourself. If you help someone, you help yourself. Blood and bone are in all people. The heart and intent matter. All life is everywhere.

Whatever religious belief you have followed, whether it is Christian, Muslim, Hindu, or Jewish, there is truth and love in God's word in every text and prayer. Make God and prayer first in your priorities of life. The boundaries you make will be easier, and there will be more joy, peace, and happiness.

68

It takes practice to become more at-one, more honest, more in-tune with yourself.

69

To have a life of living with God and His love, there are three basic principles: discipline, devotion, and introspection.

70

Our personality requires discipline for self-control of our physical desires for food, sex, love, and other worldly objects.

71

Connecting with God through prayer and introspection builds confidence, detachment from worldly objects, inner strength, and compassion.

72

Devotion is love and a way of life in which we let go of the physical world and walk in the presence of God.

73

Remember the first commandment requiring us to love God with all our heart, all our soul, and all our mind.

74

It is this unconditional and unreserved love for God that leads to the care for our neighbor.

75

Go inside in devotion; a humbleness of the spirit appears, and a connectedness to the Holy Spirit begins to take place.

76

With loving devotion, all anxieties, depressions, and worries of the world are gone and replaced with a tender loving.

77

Prayer is a way to stay centered in the gentle, sweet happiness of your heart and the wisdom of intuitive knowing.

78

God and Jesus are intimate friends. Each day when I pray and meditate, I see them inside my creative imagination.

79

Affirm each day that God loves you and gives you all good things, that you love Him and do the things He wants you to do.

80

Share a situation or a person with Him, and ask for a way to know and understand how to handle a particular situation.

81

In your mind and heart, God is everywhere and in everything. All things come from God, so give thanks for all you have.

82

Ask to be of service in His name; surrender in loving trust to His loving care, knowing He brings all good things.

83

Ask through Him for health, wealth, and happiness through opportunities of loving, caring, and sharing.

84

God is not the bellhop in the sky to deliver every whim or wish. To let go is to let go of the false pride of "I Know."

85

Surrender the rationalizing (rationing lies) of your life to the truth of what's really going on.

86

Don't resist your negative
thoughts and feelings;
instead, embrace
them, and ask
God to show you what
the lesson might be.

87

God does more
than hear words,
He reads our hearts.
Jesus taught that
all good and bad originates
in men's hearts.

88

Whatever religious belief, whether it is Christian, Muslim, Hindu, or Jewish, there is truth and love in God's Word.

89

Make God/prayer first in your life and the boundaries you make will be easier. There will be more joy, peace, and happiness.

You have no need to travel anywhere. Journey within yourself, enter a mine of rubies and bathe in the splendor of your own Light.

RUMI

SECTION VIII

IMAGE

Imagine that each person born is innocent and naïve to the world. As we grow, we learn that the law of cause and effect and our attitude have a great deal to do with how we experience our life: "as a man thinketh in his heart, he becomes," and as a result, we develop a personality or self-image.

The way I spell image: I Am A God Energized Being. We are spiritual beings having a human experience. We are made of God's Light and filled with God's loving energy. Our body is a sacred temple living in our own Garden of Eden, where we are to be honored and cared for. Our mind and emotions are energy that fill our temple and Garden like a glass that is filled with light or energy. If we lack self-esteem or have negative thoughts and feelings, such as shame, guilt, apathy, grief, fear, lust, or anger in our consciousness, our temple in the Garden of Eden develops an energy leak. I call it "leaky consciousness." If there are many feelings of unworthiness, then there are more energy leaks.

These energy leaks separate us from the wisdom (Adam/mind) and love (Eve/ heart). We are stuck either in the past, holding onto a past hurt, or in the future, trying to control the outcome of events. Often to cover up or ease the pain of the energy leaks, people will acquire addictions. Addictions of food, alcohol, drugs, sex, work, worry, and fear are all ways to mask our inner pain.

Have you noticed when you first acquire or experience them that you may feel great and satisfied, but then you distance yourself from that thing and go looking for something else to fill the lack or need? Have you ever gone to the grocery store when you were hungry? Did you buy things that you did not really need because your hunger made those things look good? Ever go out to pick up a person when you were lonely or needy inside, or go shopping at the mall with your credit cards when you felt lonely or sad?

There is a difference in taking care of our basic needs and the need we feel from a deep lack of emotional fullness or emptiness.

Whatever the goal in life, keep your eye on the donut and not the hole.

Think how often we discipline our children with negatives. Don't fall. Don't touch that. Don't... Don't... Don't. Sometimes what may seem like disobeying could just be their subconscious processing the experience of falling or touching? Have you ever thought, "I don't want to be in this job all my life," "I don't want to fail," and "I don't want to lose this sale"? Think about it. By the time your brain has got to the "don't" or "must not," your whole body has already received the message: stay in the job, fail, and miss the sale.

During my life changes, I had to recognize that part of my driven life came from seeing my life as the hole in a donut. The training of my self was a challenge as I began to break old habits. I stand guard at the door of my mind and monitor my thoughts and what I want to create.

In reflection, I can see that negative thoughts were actually keeping me from having the thing I longed for: the more I desired, the greater the resistance. I was attracting to myself like a mirror only that which I was holding in my mind and emotions. Energy is everywhere in everything, and God made everything, so He is everywhere, even in my negative thoughts. We cannot see radio or television waves, yet we can see and hear its sound and images when they go into little boxes we have in our home. We cannot see the signals of our wireless telephones, yet we can talk to people anywhere in the world. The same is true with our inner communication with God and the energy vibration and intention we transmit when we think and feel about something or someone. Have you ever thought of someone you have not heard from for some time and then receive a telephone call or letter the same day? We are all connected in God's loving threads of His Consciousness. It is tuning into the Light of the Holy Spirit that is inside and creating a connection that you can feel and learn to trust.

God has given each person certain talents and abilities, and He holds us responsible for developing them. Many times, people do not explore their own talents. They accept others' definitions of who they are, without seeking if these definitions fit. We lose ourselves when we conform to others' wishes for what we "should" be. We are separate people with separate identities. We must own what is our true self and develop it with God's grace and truth.

How can we break the never-ending cycle of our brokenheartedness, our leaky consciousness?

> "Ask, and you will be given what you ask for. Seek, and you will find. Knock, and the door will be opened. For everyone who asks, receives. Anyone who seeks, finds. If only you will knock, the door will open."
>
> **MATTHEW 7:7:8**

What is your dream? Are you a musician, perhaps a singer, who has heard that you have "no ear" and cannot sing? Music is not the only gift that can be lost or buried due to the power of negative words—sometimes an artist is not lost, just badly wounded. Sometimes our parents have parental concern over our "heartbreaks" of a creative profession. However, how much more heartbreaking is it to have a parent who squelches your dream, refuses to acknowledge your gifts, even when they are seen or appreciated by others? The power of negative words can be just as abusive as if someone were to hit you physically. How many people have jobs they have resigned themselves to because of salary-itus?

90

Each person born is innocent and naïve to the world. As we grow, we learn the law of cause and effect for our attitude.

91

We experience our life "as a man thinketh in his heart, he becomes," and as a result, we develop a personality/self-image.

92

The way I spell image: I Am A God Energized Being. We are spiritual beings having a human experience.

93

We are made of God's Light and filled with God's loving energy. Our body is a sacred temple living in our own Garden of Eden.

94

Our mind and emotions are energy that fill our body temple, and the Garden like a glass filled with Light or energy.

95

Negative thoughts, feelings, or lack of self-esteem, such as shame, guilt, grief, fear, lust, or anger, is an energy leak.

96

If there are a lot of feelings of unworthiness, then there are more light energy leaks: "leaky consciousness."

97

These energy leaks separate us from the wisdom and love in our hearts. We are stuck in the past or in the future.

98

To cover up the pain of the energy leaks, people will acquire addictions, which are ways to temporarily feel good or happy.

99

Now write: 3 things you love, 3 things you are looking forward to, and 3 things you are grateful for.

....

....

....

....

....

....

100

There is a difference between taking care of our basic needs and the need we feel from a lack of emotional fullness.

101

Whatever the goal in life, keep your eye on the donut and not the hole.

102

We often discipline our children with negatives. Don't fall. Don't touch that. Don't. Don't.

103

Ever thought, "I don't want to be in this job all my life," "I don't want to fail," and "I don't want to lose this sale"?

104

Your brain has heard the "don't" message your body has already received: fail, stay in the job, and miss the sale.

105

Negative thoughts keep you from having what you longed for; the more you desire, the greater the resistance.

106

Energy is everywhere, in everything, and God made everything, so He is everywhere, even in my negative thoughts.

107

Like the invisible waves
of light from the Internet,
we are all connected
in the loving threads of
His Consciousness.

108

It is tuning into the
Light/Holy Spirit
that is inside us and creating
a connection that you can
feel and learn to trust.

109

God has given each person certain talents and abilities, and He holds us responsible for developing them.

110

How can we break the
never-ending cycle of our
broken-heartedness
our leaky consciousness?

111

"Ask and you will be given. Seek and you will find. Knock and the door will be opened." Matthew 7:7:8

112

What is your dream? Are you a musician? Perhaps a singer who heard that you have "no ear" and cannot sing?

113

Gifts can be lost or buried due to the power of negative words; an artist is not lost, just badly wounded.

114

The power of negative words can be just as abusive as if someone were to hit you physically.

115

When we feel honest and courageous, we can see the fears of the unknown and yet see possibilities of something new.

116

If you were to be honest about your life, what dream do you have in your heart that wants to be expressed?

I AM — two of the most powerful words. For what you put after them shapes your reality.

M E

SECTION IX

My Name Is I AM

We are creatures bound by physical needs, laws, and limitations, yet we are also conscious co-creators of life who exude unlimited possibilities with every thought, movement, feeling, and intent.

To change and direct ourselves takes a clear and strong intention. Like computers, we are programmed to be who and what we are. Our mind is the hardware of the computer, while the software or programs that our mind runs come from the experiences we have had during our lifetime.

We have years of programming from our family, friends, education, television, movies, and music. Each moment, we are being programmed by something. It often takes feeling disturbed with where we are in our familiar place to overcome our resistance.

A way to redirect the darkness into the light is to bring the highest and fastest frequencies of the Holy Spirit into the lower and slower frequencies; in that way, we are able to nullify and dissipate what we have come to know as our energy leaks. Like computers, we are programmed to be who and what we are. With a strong intention and direction, we increase the likelihood to change the inner programming. We overcome our resistance to our familiar thoughts and feelings of being out of control.

To create change, we will be using a perspective that takes us out of time as we know it.♥ I believe that we have time in the physical world so everything does not happen at once. However, in our mind, emotions, and unconscious, there is no time. Our mind and emotions can be thinking about something in the past at the same time we are experiencing something in the present. When I think of myself singing in the present, I can also be aware of an incident in my childhood in which my parents said I was not good enough. With the feelings of rejection in that past memory, I might not be able to sing with the depth of my heart.

To heal the wound of the past, we must go out of time, past the personality, to the sacred part of us.

♥ Time as defined by *Webster's Ninth New Collegiate Dictionary* is, "the measured or measurable period during which an action, process, or condition exists or continues."

Surely, no word or phrase is less understood or more critical to comprehension of the Bible story than **"I AM."** In addition, he said, 'I am the God of your father, the God of Abraham, the God of Isaac, and the God of Jacob.' Then Moses said to God, "If I come to the people of Israel and say to them, 'The God of your fathers has sent me to you,' and they ask me, 'What is his name?' "Say this to the people of Israel: 'The LORD, the God of your fathers, the God of Abraham, the God of Isaac, and the God of Jacob, has sent me to you.' This is my name for ever, and thus I am to be remembered throughout all generations..."

"Know thyself." This passage, "I AM THE I AM," can be understood only when it is seen that Moses stood at a critical point in human evolution when the ego, mind, emotions, and unconscious was making its transition from group or tribal soul to individual soul. Moses himself was gifted with the ancient and atavistic clairvoyance, and could not bring himself fully into the era of the developing "I AM," hence he could not fully recognize it in the wilderness (Exodus 17, 6; Numbers 20, 11-12; Deuteronomy 32; 1 Corinthians 10, 4) When we say, "I AM," we are in the present, our soul energy is being called forward, and we are beginning to KNOW who we are from the inner sacred part of us. Invoking this energy can lift and change the inner consciousness and experience the sacredness of who we truly are.

As we reawaken our creative imagination with introspection and discernment, the kingdom of heaven that is within can be experienced. Each person has the ability to tap in, utilize, and direct it. Energy follows thought. As we become aware of how we are thinking, we can see how what we put out comes back. Then we can observe that what we focus on and put energy into is what we get. Through observation, we can learn more about what we are doing and make a choice to change because we are creators.

In the next chapter, you are going to fill the energy leaks in your temple and Garden of Eden by using the intention of "I AM." We are going to do a process based on neutral observation, trust, and awareness. Change does not have to be hard or scary. Let us remember that every experience we have had or will have is one of learning. Little by little, we will be removing judgments and elements of power and outward control. Right now, we are learning how to trust our self and the inner part of us that wants to heal and be whole. We are creating our own ten acres in our Garden of Eden from a sacred place of "I AM."

117

We are creatures bound by physical needs, laws, and limitations and are co-creators of life, exuding unlimited possibilities.

118

To change and direct ourselves takes a clear and strong intention. Like computers, we are programmed to be what we are.

119

Our mind is the hardware of the computer; the software our mind runs comes from our experiences.

120

Years of input from our family, friends, education, television, movies, music, you name it — each moment, we're programmed.

121

It often takes feeling disturbed with where we are in our familiar place to overcome our resistance.

122

Redirect the darkness into the light; bring the highest frequencies of the Holy Spirit into the lower frequencies.

123

With a strong intention and direction, we increase the likelihood of changing the inner programming.

124

Time is in the physical world so everything does not happen at once. In our mind, emotions and unconscious have no time.

125

Imagine singing in the present; also be aware of an incident in childhood when you were told you were not good enough.

126

With the feelings of rejection in a past memory, you might not be able to sing with the depth of your heart.

127

To heal the wound of the past, we must go out of time, past the personality, to the sacred part of us: the " I AM."

128

Fill the energy leaks in your temple and Garden of Eden by using the intention of "I AM."

129

Change does not have to be hard or scary. Create your own ten acres in your Garden of Eden from a sacred place of "I AM."

*If you can dream
it, you can do it.*

WALT DISNEY

SECTION X

Five Keys to Realizing Your Dream

Like it or not, life and living is about movement, advancement, and change. People are nonliving when angry, depressed, and feeling sorry for themselves or filled with fear. It is okay to try out negative emotions and how they feel, but it is not a place one would wisely want to stay. In the world as a classroom, we get to see how it feels to be happy or sad, jealous or grateful, but you are supposed to learn from the experience and ultimately figure out which feels painful and which feels great. The healing of ourselves is to heal the wounded, diseased, and injured, where we have separated ourselves from the eternal beingness.

In this next exercise, you will find where the fear, anger, and depression are in your dream. Keep in mind that the feelings and emotions are just energy leaks. We are going out of gear, observing our mind and emotions as we move through our inner resistance. In stating your dream, how do you feel? Be aware of the feelings attached to what you are asking for. There is a list of questions to ask yourself to see where your resistance may be in what you are dreaming to have.

Realize Your Dream — 10 Minutes a Day in 30 Days

KEY ONE — WRITE YOUR DREAM

In reflection of your dream, ask yourself the following questions to see where the resistance could be for you to have your dream.

After each question, see if you feel any resistance; if you feel clear, go to the next question.

1. Is it possible for someone to? Not just you, someone?
2. Is it possible for me to?
3. Is it okay for me to?
4. Am I worthy to have or express this?
5. Is it safe for me to?
6. I deserve to.
7. I am permitted to.
8. I can.
9. I now am (doing) (having) (being)?
10. I am certain I am (doing) (having) (being)?

KEY TWO — ALIGN YOUR BODY, MIND, AND SOUL

Did you feel clear through the list of questions, or were there one or more questions where you felt unclear? The inner feelings to have your dream could be very overwhelming at this point. That is okay. Just allow the experience to be. Which of the questions had the most resistance? Was it feeling safe, or maybe it was feeling worthy? We are going to work with feeling safe or worthy.

Now take the negative feeling and make it into a positive statement. To heal the wound of the past, we must embrace the negative, go past the personality to the sacred part of us, I AM.

When we say, "I AM," we are in the present, our soul energy is being called forward, and we are beginning to KNOW who we are from the sacred inner part of us.

Write this statement:

I, *your name*, AM now safe (or worthy) to have (do or be) (my dream) of (fill in the blank).

At the end of the affirmative statement, also include easily, pleasurably, safely, with fun, joy, and enthusiasm, for the Highest Good of All Concerned.

Remember, our intent of how we direct our self is very important. We always use "for the Highest Good of All Concerned" because if after going through the process of clearing, you still do not have what you want, it probably was not for the highest good. In some situations, what you want could be coming in, just not in *your* timeframe. Surrendering, letting go, and letting God is important. For some people, the dream may be opening you to receive something else that is even better and greater—the process of opening you to a sense of serendipity — you go out for one experience and find a better choice.

After you have written the affirmation, then write all of the negative thoughts and feelings you may have that are in the way of you having your dream. Just let go; remember, it is energy that needs to be released and let go.

KEY THREE — FORGIVENESS

Have you written all of the negative thoughts and feelings to where you feel empty inside? Good, now take the negative thoughts and feelings you have written and either burn them (in a safe place, like over the kitchen sink) or throw them away where you cannot see them again.

Next, you are going to fill the empty void with God's loving. Just now, find a comfortable chair to sit in. Relax with your arms and hands uncrossed. Then visualize in your mind the Light of God surrounding, filling, and protecting you for the highest good and just ask, "Father Mother God, I ask just now to be surrounded, filled, and protected by your highest and most loving light." Now ask for guidance in having your dream come true. Listen.

Perhaps there are situations where forgiveness for yourself and others need to be done; if so, just ask, "Father Mother God, I ask just now that I forgive myself in judging myself (in the situation, or with) (fill in the blank). And I forgive (the person in the situation) for judging me."

Let go of any mental or emotional baggage at this time. Give it up to God and the Holy Spirit inside of you. See yourself, your past situations, and those you were involved with in perfect Light and unconditional loving.

When you feel complete, come back into your awareness in the room. Write down your experience.

KEY FOUR — AFFIRM WHO YOU ARE
Now write:
1. Three things you love
2. Three things you are looking forward to
3. Three things you are grateful for

How do you feel now? Do you feel uplifted and connected inside, where your heart, mind, and emotions are all going into a positive direction? Great! You are on your way to having your dream or the one God wants for you.

KEY FIVE — 30 DAY PRACTICE
Continue to do this process, asking yourself the questions listed in Key One, where you experience the resistance to your dream each day for at least 30 days. It takes the practice of disciplining yourself each day and your attitude toward your dream that determines whether you are successful.

After a week of doing the process of creating your dream, go back to the list of priorities, and see if your priorities have changed.

Testimonial
After the death of my husband two years ago, I was on a continual search for recreating myself. It seemed that the path I was on had led me to a place that I never wanted

to be: alone without the love of my life. Then I resigned my career position to develop my own consulting company, but along the way, I was mugged and all my identity stolen—twice, no less. Next was six months of total focus on nothing but repairing all the chaos that a theft ring had created. My new career was Identity Theft.

Grace Allison and her book, *A Dream Is a Wish the Heart Makes*, the manual and workshop, were the perfect vehicles in assisting me to honor what was and embrace what would come. Through this beautiful process that she has so carefully prepared, I found peace . . . I was released to enter into a new future filled with possibilities.

Truly, I emerged from the darkness into the Light. Immediately, my life changed. No more fear, no more "wandering in the desert" . . . my life had focus, joy, and I was empowered to move on. With lightning speed, the chaos stopped . . . I let go of the grief . . . love presented itself again in the form of an amazing man who was drawn to my spirit . . .to the Joy, Laughter, Enthusiasm, and Energy. I was not "looking" for love, yet it came to me. I attracted this gift because the "blocks" in my spirit were gone. To experience love so deeply in a lifetime is a treasured gift. To experience it twice is nothing short of awesome and quite humbling. I am at Peace. I AM.

Do You Have a Dream is a continuing process . . . a joyful adventure that I apply and work through daily. Sandi deVeau.

130

Like it or not, life and living is about movement, advancement, and change.

131

Go out of gear; observe your mind and emotions as you move through your inner resistance.

132

Write: I, (your name), AM now safe (or worthy) to have (do or be) (my dream) of (fill in the blank).

133

At the end of the statement,
include easily, pleasurably,
safely, and with fun,
joy and enthusiasm for
the Highest Good.

134

After you have written the affirmation, then write all the negative thoughts you have in the way of you having your dream.

....

....

....

....

....

....

135

Take the written negative thoughts and feelings, and either burn them or throw them away where you cannot see them again.

136

Next, you will fill the empty void with God's love. Find a comfortable chair to sit in. Relax.

137

Visualize in your mind the Light of God surrounding, filling, and protecting you for the highest good.

138

Now ask for guidance in having your dream come true. Listen.

139

Forgiveness: "Father, Mother God, I ask just now that I forgive myself in judging myself."

140

"And I forgive (the person in the situation) for judging me."

ABOUT THE AUTHOR

Grace Allison is a successful award-winning author who has assisted hundreds to discover their spiritual power in order to meet their everyday challenges. She is a modern mystic, wellness consultant, business development adviser, marketing coach, and workshop facilitator. She has faced many life challenges, including a life-threatening disease, and used what she encountered as a stimulus to gain greater happiness and fulfillment. She lives in Lubbock, Texas with her husband, John Blair, and maintains a private health and success coaching practice.

ACT NOW!

Send an email to *Grace@ModernMysticMedia.com* and write in the subject line, "Do You Have a Dream." By doing so, you will receive a free two-minute meditation in my voice and a free copy of the award-winning e-book, *A Dream Is a Wish the Heart Makes: Or If at First You Don't Succeed, Change the Rules.*

To learn more about Grace Allison, Modern Mystic, go to *Grace@ModernMysticMedia.com*. Discover her new science- fiction thriller, *Einstein's Compass: A Novel of What If?* and register for a free chapter of the book, to be released in spring 2017.

Find Grace Allison's books on Bublish, where you can read chapterbubbles of her books and buy them on the spot. Enjoy this #AuthorProfile:

http://bit.ly/28SXsgZ
VIA @BUBLISHME.

www.ingramcontent.com/pod-product-compliance
Lightning Source LLC
Chambersburg PA
CBHW070611300426
44113CB00010B/1489